THE FARMINGTON COMMUNITY LIBRARY
FARMINGTON HILLS BRANCH
32737 WEST TWELVE MILE ROAD
FARMINGTON HILLS, MI 48334-3302
(248) 553-0300

MAR 16 2011

W9-CNA-863

Rosa's Bus

Jo S. Kittinger
Illustrated by Steven Walker

CALKINS CREEK
HONESDALE, PENNSYLVANIA

30036010725479

The author and illustrator wish to thank Angela Hall, vice president, Birmingham Civil Rights Institute, Birmingham, Alabama, and Georgette Norman, director, Rosa Parks Museum, Troy University, Montgomery, Alabama, for their gracious assistance.

Text copyright © 2010 by Jo S. Kittinger
Illustrations copyright © 2010 by Steven Walker
All rights reserved

CALKINS CREEK
An Imprint of Boyds Mills Press, Inc.
815 Church Street
Honesdale, Pennsylvania 18431
Printed in the United States of America

CIP data is available.

First edition
The text of this book is set in 16-point Minion Pro.
The illustrations are done in oils.

10 9 8 7 6 5 4 3 2 1

For Rick, my wonderful husband, because he hates injustice
—J.K.

A special thanks to my mom and dad
—S.W.

When Bus #2857 rolled off
    the assembly line in 1948,
no one cheered,
no one paid attention,
no one knew that one day
    Bus #2857 would be famous.

The bus left the General Motors factory in Michigan
and headed for Terre Haute, Indiana,
where it carried folks for several years
before moving south to Alabama in 1954.

Around the time the bus arrived in Montgomery,
the U.S. Supreme Court in Washington, D.C.,
ruled that separate schools for black children
    and white children were unequal.
The civil rights movement was beginning to roll.

Welcome
to
Montgomery

By now, Bus #2857 was six years old.
Its yellow paint had faded some,
but inside, ten seats back,
there was a newly painted, movable sign.
It read: *Colored*.

White people climbed aboard Bus #2857,
paid a dime, and took a seat in the front of the bus.
Black people climbed aboard the bus, paid a dime,
but often had to walk back down the steps
and go to the rear door—
even if it was raining,
even if their legs were broken,
even if they were cold and the steps were hard to climb.
That's just the way things were.

Whites sat up front, "colored" in back.
Black people were called colored
    back then.
That's just the way things were.

When the "white" seats filled,
an entire row of black people
    had to stand up
so one white person could sit down.
Black people weren't allowed to share a
row with white people.
That's just the way things were.

If black people didn't stand up,
the bus driver could have them arrested,
and they'd have to pay a fine.
Those were the rules,
    called Jim Crow laws.
That's just the way things were.

Bus #2857 traveled the streets of Montgomery,
carrying people to work,
to church,
and to the store.
Black people needed the bus.
The bus company needed black people to ride.
Jingle-jangle, dime upon dime—
dimes kept the buses in business.

On the evening of December 1, 1955,
a winter day like any other,
Bus #2857 chugged along the streets,
stopping at corners,
brakes screeching,
doors hissing.

Mrs. Rosa Parks boarded the bus.
After a long day of sewing and pressing clothes,
she took a seat behind the sign.
At the next stop,
all the front seats were filled,
and a white man was left standing.

The bus driver motioned for Rosa
and three other black passengers in her row
    to stand up,
so the white man could sit down.
Three passengers did as the driver ordered.
Rosa sat still.

The busload of people
moaned and groaned,
anxious to get home.
The driver said, "Move,
or I'll have you arrested."
Still Rosa sat.
That winter day
the police took Rosa to jail.

Did you hear?
Did you hear?
Rosa was arrested!

The news raced around town like a field on fire.
Meetings were held in homes and at churches.
Black leaders had been waiting for this moment—
waiting for something to happen on the buses,
something that would give people the courage
    to change the way things were.
They printed flyers that read:

Please stay off all buses on Monday!

On Monday morning,
when Bus #2857 pulled up to its first stop,
few black faces were among those who
    climbed aboard.

The same was true for every bus in Montgomery
at every stop that day.
A bus boycott had begun,
led by a young minister named Dr. Martin Luther King, Jr.
He said, "The great glory of American
    democracy is the right to protest for right."

Black people throughout the city vowed to avoid riding the buses
until no one could tell them to move from their seats.

The bus boycott lasted a week,
then a month.
Black people walked to work,
to church,
and to the store.
Their feet got sore,
but still they walked.
Some people who had cars
    offered rides to others.
Black taxi drivers offered special fares,
until they were stopped
    by those Jim Crow laws.

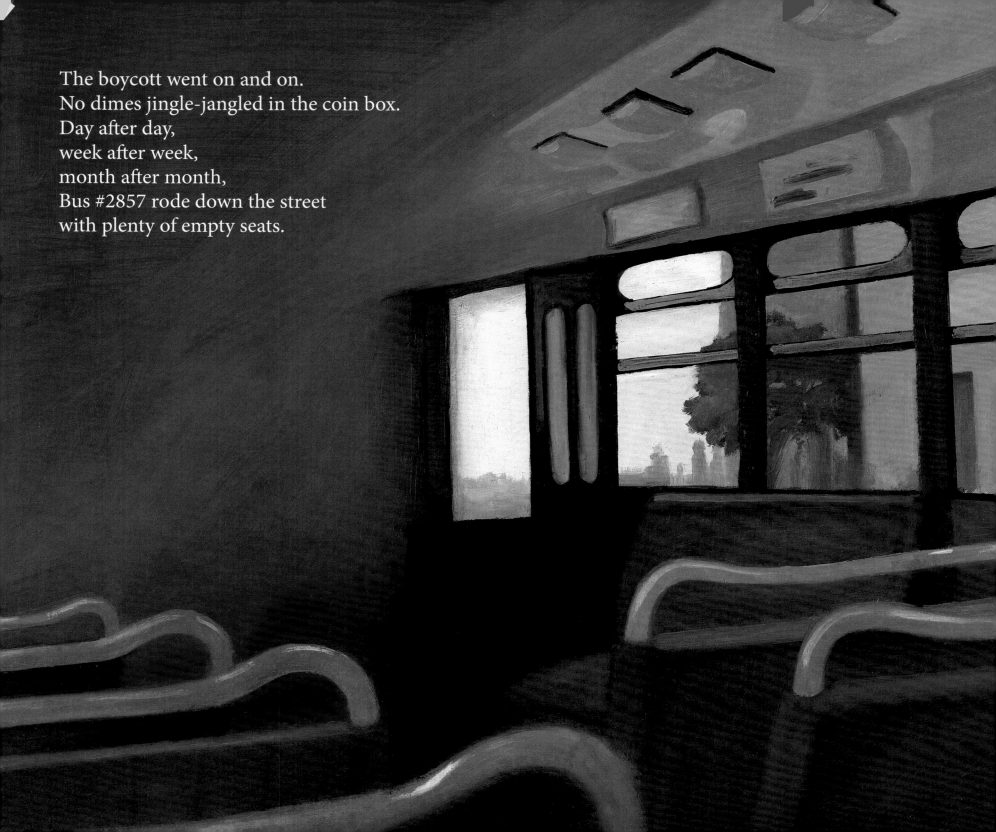

The boycott went on and on.
No dimes jingle-jangled in the coin box.
Day after day,
week after week,
month after month,
Bus #2857 rode down the street
with plenty of empty seats.

Black people walked
and walked,
wearing holes in the soles
    of their shoes.
They walked for 382 days.
That's how long they boycotted
    the buses.
A year after the boycott began,
the Supreme Court
    in Washington, D.C., ruled
that the way things were in
    Montgomery must change.
Black people could no longer be
    forced to give up their seats for
    white people.
They could sit in any seat they
    wanted on the bus.
The civil rights movement had
    won an important victory.

Bus #2857 was full again.

It ran many more years
    on the streets of Montgomery
as the civil rights movement rolled on and on.

Then the city replaced its old buses
with ones that were shiny and new.
Bus #2857 was put out of service.

A man bought the old bus to save it
    from the junkyard.
Summer and winter,
year after year,
Bus #2857 sat in a field.
The engine got ripped out,
and windows got broken.
Instead of people,
the old bus held tools and lumber.
A pine tree dripped sap on the roof.
Its metal rusted.
Bus #2857 had been forgotten—
or so it seemed.

Donnie Williams remembered.
He owned the bus in the field.
Mr. Williams waited half his life—
more than thirty years—
for the right time,
a time when people cared enough about the bus
to clean off the sap,
scrape off the rust,
and replace the broken windows.

Fifty-five years after it rolled off the assembly line,
Bus #2857 returned to Michigan.
This time, people cheered when the bus
rolled into the Henry Ford Museum.

Today Bus #2857 welcomes people of all colors—
those who remember the days when they sat behind the sign,
and those who sat in front.

It welcomes people who remember
    the way things were
and people who only have heard the stories.
Think about Bus #2857—
imagine where it has been
and where we have yet to go.

Henry Ford Museum

About the Bus

Manufacturer: General Motors Corporation, Pontiac, Michigan
Built: March 1948
Model Number: DH-3610
Serial Number: 1132
Coach Identification Number: 2857
Capacity: 36 passengers
Engine: Diesel engine with hydraulic transmission
Service: Terre Haute, Indiana, 1948–1954; Montgomery, Alabama, 1954–1971

After the bus was retired from service, it was sold as surplus in 1971 to Roy H. Summerford, who realized its historical value. The bus was inherited by Summerford's daughter and son-in-law, Vivian and Donnie Williams. In 2001, the bus was purchased at auction by the Henry Ford Museum. It took nearly five months to restore the bus. Great care was taken to have the bus look as it did when Rosa Parks held her seat—from the golden paint to the red Alabama dirt on the wheels. On February 1, 2003, Bus #2857 went on permanent display at the Henry Ford Museum, Dearborn, Michigan. You can learn more at www.thehenryford.org/exhibits/rosaparks/default.asp.

Author's Note

Rosa Parks's simple act of refusing to give up her seat on a bus, so that a row of seats would be open for white passengers, started a wave of protests that rolled across the United States. Protests led to lawsuits, and the resulting court decisions changed the way that black people and people of all races would be treated in our nation. But Rosa Parks, now known as the mother of the civil rights movement, was not the first person to get in trouble for disobeying a bus driver in Montgomery, Alabama.

Most every rider could tell stories of how they had been mistreated or spoken to rudely. But real fear jumped aboard the buses in 1950 when Thomas Edward Brooks, a twenty-year-old African American soldier, refused a bus driver's order to get off the bus through the front door and reenter through the rear door. A policeman who arrived at the scene hit Mr. Brooks with his billy club and attempted to drag him off the bus. When Mr. Brooks broke free and ran from the bus, the policeman shot and killed him. The police called it self-defense rather than murder.

On March 2, 1955, Claudette Colvin, a fifteen-year-old high-school student, was arrested when she refused to give up her seat for a white passenger. Later, on October 21, 1955, Mary Louise Smith, age nineteen, was arrested when she refused a bus driver's order to move for a white woman.

When Rosa Parks was arrested on December 1, 1955, black leaders decided to make their stand. Everyone who knew Mrs. Parks respected her kind, gentle manner. She had been active in groups such as the National Association for the Advancement of Colored People (NAACP) and the Women's Political Council, seeking to change the way black people were treated. She was friends with many black leaders in the community, such as E. D. Nixon and Jo Ann Robinson. The time had come for a bus boycott.

While the black community fought for change by boycotting city buses, lawyers battled in the courts. The bus boycott ended December 20, 1956, when the U.S. Supreme Court, in a case called *Browder v. Gayle*, ruled that segregation of Montgomery's buses violated the Constitution of the United States.

Sources

Books

Brinkley, Douglas. *Rosa Parks*. New York: Viking, 2000.

Donovan, Sandy. *Rosa Parks*. African-American Biographies. Chicago: Raintree, 2004.

Dubowski, Cathy East. *Rosa Parks: Don't Give In!* New York: Bearport Publishing, 2006.

Friese, Kai Jabir. *Rosa Parks: The Movement Organizes*. Englewood Cliffs, NJ: Silver Burdett Press, 1990.

Gelsi, Teresa. *Rosa Parks and the Montgomery Bus Boycott*. Brookfield, CT: Millbrook Press, 1991.

Greenfield, Eloise. *Rosa Parks*. New York: Thomas Y. Crowell, 1973.

Parks, Rosa. *Rosa Parks: My Story*. With Jim Haskins. New York: Dial Books, 1992.

Siegel, Beatrice. *The Year They Walked: Rosa Parks and the Montgomery Bus Boycott*. New York: Four Winds Press, 1992.

Web Sites

(Active at time of publication)

Africanaonline. Black History. www.africanaonline.com/montgomery.htm.

Feeney, Mark. "Rosa Parks, Civil Rights Icon, Dead at 92." *Boston Globe*, October 25, 2005. www.boston.com/news/nation/articles/2005/10/25/rosa_parks_civil_rights_icon_dead_at_92/?page=3.

Harmon, Rick. "E. D. Nixon." *Montgomery Advertiser*. www.montgomeryboycott.com/profile_nixon.htm.

National Center for Public Policy Research. www.nationalcenter.org/brown.html. Supreme Court of the United States. *Brown v. Board of Education*, 347 U.S. 483 (1954).

Rosa and Raymond Parks Institute for Self Development."Rosa Louise Parks Biography." www.rosaparks.org/bio.html.

Time magazine. "The Time 100." www.time.com/time/time100/heroes/profile/parks01.html.

Interviews

Donnie Williams, previous owner of Bus #2857. Interviews, 2006 and 2007.

Further Reading

Dubois, Muriel L. *Rosa Parks*. Photo-Illustrated Biographies. Mankato, MN: Capstone Press, 2003.

Dubowski, Cathy East. *Rosa Parks: Don't Give In!* New York: Bearport Publishing, 2006.

Kishel, Ann-Marie. *Rosa Parks: A Life of Courage*. Minneapolis: Lerner Publications, 2006.

Mara, Wil. *Rosa Parks*. Rookie Biographies. New York: Children's Press/Scholastic, 2003.

Parks, Rosa. *Rosa Parks: My Story*. With Jim Haskins. New York: Dial Books, 1992.

Ringgold, Faith. *If a Bus Could Talk: The Story of Rosa Parks*. New York: Simon and Schuster Books for Young Readers, 1999.

Web Sites of Interest

(Active at time of publication)

Ferris State University. Jim Crow Museum of Racist Memorabilia. www.ferris.edu/jimcrow/menu.htm.

Henry Ford Museum. www.hfmgv.org/museum; www.hfmgv.org/exhibits/rosaparks/default.asp.

Rosa and Raymond Parks Institute for Self Development. www.rosaparks.org/bio.html.